5to

FRIENDS
OF ACPL

D1248939

UNUSUAL PARTNERS

Symbiosis in the Living World

UNUSUAL PARTNERS

Symbiosis in the Living World

by Alvin and Virginia B. Silverstein

illustrated by Mel Hunter

McGRAW-HILL BOOK COMPANY

New York · Toronto · London · Sydney

For Robert Alan Silverstein

Copyright © 1968 by Alvin and Virginia B. Silverstein. All Rights Reserved. Printed in the United States of America. No part of this publication may be reproduced, stored in a retrieval system, or transmitted, in any form or by any means, electronic, mechanical, photocopying, recording, or otherwise, without the prior written permission of the publisher.

Library of Congress Catalog Card Number: 68–25667

1234567890 HDBP 7543210698

Contents

CO. SCHOOLS
C719119

1

Living
and Working
Together

In the world of nature there are many strange relationships.   We do not find it very surprising that animal families often stay together while the young are being raised, or even that some animals of the same kind, such as cattle or elephants, live together in herds.   But it does seem odd that quite different kinds of animals or plants are often found living together in such a way that at least one of them benefits from the association.

In Africa, a small, dull-colored bird called the honey guide and a stubby-legged, slow-moving animal called the honey badger or ratel often work together in a kind of partnership, with profit for both.

The honey guide, a member of the woodpecker family, loves to eat the larvae or worm-like young of bees, wasps, and termites, and it also enjoys feasting on bits

A ratel follows a honey guide to a prize of honey for both.

of waxy honeycomb.   But though the honey guide, flying
about through the forest, is very good at finding bees'
nests, it has no way to open them by itself, to get at
the honeycomb inside.

The ratel, a member of the weasel family, loves to eat
honey, and it also finds bees and other insects an excel-
lent addition to its usual diet of frogs, snakes, and rats.
The ratel is very well equipped to steal honey from bee-
hives.   Its long, heavy fur and thick, tough skin protect
it from the stings of angry bees, and its forepaws are
furnished with strong, long claws, which can easily tear
an insect nest open.   But the ratel is so slow-moving

8

that it would take too long for it to go searching through the forest for bees' nests.

It would seem that if this pair, the honey guide and the ratel, could work together as a team, there would be a nice profit for each. And this is exactly what happens.

When a honey guide spots a wild bees' nest, or perhaps a great earthen mound built by a colony of termites, it flies about looking for a ratel. As soon as it finds one, it flutters excitedly about the animal's head, chirping shrilly. The ratel begins to follow, as the bird flies off for a few feet. Then the bird stops and dances about, chirping, to be sure that its animal partner is just behind. On the honey guide leads, until they reach the nest.

Now it is the ratel's turn to go to work. With its strong claws it tears open the nest, and begins to devour bees and honey. The honey guide waits patiently for the ratel to break open the honeycomb. When it does, then it is the bird's turn to feast.

If a honey guide that has located a bees' nest cannot find a ratel, it may try to lead some other animal, such as a baboon, to the prize. Even humans that live nearby have learned to follow this keen-eyed bird. Both animals and man have found that partnership with the honey guide can be quite profitable indeed.

The honey guide also forms two other, and quite different, kinds of associations with different kinds of creatures. Most animals cannot digest wax at all, and the honey guide is no exception. But millions of bacteria, creatures so small that they cannot be seen without a microscope, live in its intestines and break down the wax into simple chemicals that the bird can digest. This too is a profitable association for both partners. The bacteria obtain food and shelter, and the honey guide can now get nourishment from the wax.

But the honey guide's third relationship is a rather one-sided one. The female bird does not build a nest and sit on her eggs and feed her young, the way other members of the woodpecker family do. Instead she finds a sheltered nest made by some other kind of woodpecker and lays a single white egg of her own inside when the other mother is not about. Soon the honey guide egg hatches, and the young bird comes out of its egg shell. It is blind and hungry and almost helpless, but it has two sharp hooks on its bill. With these it bites the other nestlings to death. Now the young honey guide can have all the food that the hard-working woodpecker mother brings, and it grows quickly. This is indeed a one-sided "partnership." Only one partner, the honey guide, gets any benefit at all. The other, the woodpecker, is actually harmed. The mother woodpecker must work hard to gather food for a baby that does not even belong to her, while her own young have been killed.

There are many different kinds of strange associations in the living world. In some cases, such as the honey guide and its bacteria, different kinds of creatures actually live together, with one or both benefiting from the association; in other cases they merely come together from time to time and cooperate, like the honey guide and the ratel. Scientists have given a name to partnerships in which creatures of different kinds live or work together, and one or both gain benefits they could not have alone. This name is symbiosis, from two Greek words meaning "a living together." There are several different types of symbiosis.

Cases in which there is benefit for both partners are called *mutualism,* since there is a mutual gain. An example is the partnership of the honey guide and the ratel, in which both profit.

In some cases, however, only one partner seems to benefit. Perhaps the other is neither helped nor harmed by the association. For instance, the orchid plant does not harm the tree on which it grows; it merely uses the tree as a platform to hold it up above the dense jungle growth. Such cases are called *commensalism.*

But in other cases of one-sided associations, one partner benefits while the other partner is harmed. Such unequal relationships are known as *parasitism.* The creature that benefits is the parasite, and the other creature at whose expense it lives is known as its host. The honey guide acts as a parasite upon other types of woodpeckers when she lays her eggs in their nests. Disease germs that grow in our bodies, gaining nourishment while they make us ill, are also parasites. So are fleas and ticks, small creatures which cling to animals' skin and suck their blood.

The word "symbiosis" was first used late in the nineteenth century by a German scientist, Heinrich de Bary, when it was discovered that two different kinds of plants can live and work together for the benefit of both. These are the lichens. They are hardy forms of plant life, which often are the first to grow in barren lands. You may find some in abandoned fields or in the woods, growing on the soil or on tree trunks. Lichens usually

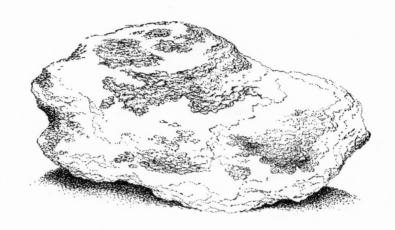

Lichens often are the first plant life to grow in barren lands.

do not grow in cities, for the soot and gases given off by factories kill them.

For centuries it was thought that a lichen was a single kind of plant. But then, when scientists studied these growths under a microscope, they discovered that lichens are really composed of two very different kinds of plants. One, an alga, is a tiny green plant, which can make its own food. The other, a fungus, is not green and cannot make its own food. The two plants depend upon each other. The alga provides enough food for both, and the fungus provides support, so that the alga can get the sunlight it needs to live and grow.

As scientists explore the world of nature, they are discovering more and more ways in which different kinds of plants and animals depend on each other and live together for the benefit of at least one of them. Sometimes the combinations are very strange indeed.

2

Cleaning
Partnerships

WHEN YOU WERE younger, your mother washed and cleaned you each day. Many kinds of animal mothers clean their young too. A lioness carefully licks each of her cubs, and a house cat washes her kittens in the same way. A mother monkey patiently picks fleas and bits of dirt from her baby's fur, and monkeys clean and groom each other even when they are grown. This helps to keep them healthy, and they seem to enjoy it.

Many animals have special cleaning problems that they cannot take care of by themselves. Even others of their kind may not be able to help them. Some of these animals form strange partnerships with other kinds of animals. These helpers actually eat bits of dirt and bothersome pests, such as insects, worms, and fungus growths, off the bodies of their larger partners.

The partnership is not one-sided. The cleaners gain a nourishing meal—for they find the pests that they remove quite good to eat. The animals that they clean gain too, for the pests are not only annoying, but often make them ill.

Sometimes the cleaning partners are strange pairs indeed. The fierce crocodiles of the Nile River in Africa and small dainty birds called plovers are a good example of this sort of partnership.

The huge crocodiles who live along the Nile are vicious man-eaters. The natives fear them, and kill them whenever they can.

The Egyptian plovers, small long-legged birds that look something like sandpipers, live on the mud flats and marshes along the Nile. Surprisingly, they do not fear the mighty crocodiles at all. In fact, the plovers and crocodiles help each other.

Small, worm-like leeches often fasten themselves tightly to the gums of the crocodiles by means of little suction cups, and suck the crocodiles' blood. The croc-

Fearlessly the tiny plovers feed inside the crocodile's mouth.

odiles do not like these leeches, but they cannot shake them free, and they have no way to pick them off. The plovers *do* like the leeches—they like to eat them.

So the mighty crocodile and the tiny plover form an unusual partnership. The crocodile opens its enormous mouth wide, and plovers flutter right into it. There within the gaping jaws they safely hop about, pulling off leeches and gobbling them down. They are not afraid of the crocodile's wicked-looking teeth. For the crocodile will wait patiently until they are finished before it again closes its powerful jaws.

The plovers help the crocodiles in another way too. They often perch nearby and with their sharp eyes keep a watch for enemies. If one approaches, they give a warning cry, and the crocodiles can dive to safety.

Another small bird, the tickbird, rides about on the broad back of the African rhinoceros, and chirps a warning if danger is near. This is a great help to the rhino, for it cannot see nearly as well as its sharp-eyed little partner.

Their meal complete, the plovers keep guard.

Tickbirds find plentiful food on the hide of the rhinoceros.

The tickbird gains from the partnership too. Perched high up on the rhino's back, it is safe from most enemies. It gets its meals there too, feeding very well on small blood-sucking parasites called ticks, which it picks from the rhino's baggy hide.

Cleaning partnerships are also very common in the waters of the world. Ferocious fish, such as sharks and barracudas, with razor-sharp teeth, usually gobble down almost any small fish they meet. But they rest quietly in the water while some very special smaller fish clean them.

There are many different kinds of these little cleaner fish. But they are all brightly colored and easy to see in the clear waters where they live. The four-eyed butterfly fish, for example, is a bright yellow fish, a few inches long. It gets its name from a pair of false eyes—round dark spots near its tail. Another kind of small cleaner fish, the wrasse (pronounced "rass"), has a pattern of dark stripes that is very easy for the larger fish to recognize.

In the Indian Ocean, the South Seas, and the Caribbean, in the warm waters near coral reefs, a regular business is carried on between little cleaner fish and the various kinds of larger fish who are their "clients." First the brightly colored little cleaners dance about a client fish, announcing that they are ready to work. The client soon slows down and rests quietly in the water, so that the little cleaners can get to work. Sometimes business is so good that there is even a waiting line. Client fish mill around, waiting for their turn to be cleaned. They may be so eager to be next that they fight among themselves.

It is an amazing sight to see a tiny cleaner fish nibbling

A fierce shark waits patiently while tiny wrasse clean its teeth.

away at a large fish's scales. It darts back and forth, eating off bits of dirt and fungus growths, pulling off parasites, and cleaning sores that might otherwise become infected.

Even the fiercest client fish lie quietly while the cleaner fish is working. The dreaded moray eel, which lurks in nooks and crannies of coral reefs and is feared by most other fish, will let a tiny wrasse or other cleaner fish nibble at its leathery skin. These daring little fish dart straight into a shark's mouth and work their way down its throat. They need not fear that they will be bitten or swallowed, for they are welcome workers.

Is all this cleaning really necessary? Indeed it is! The partnership is just as important to the client fish as it is to the little cleaners that get their meals by removing dirt and parasites from their larger neighbors. One scientist found out just how important this cleaning symbiosis can be, by removing all the cleaner fish from a small coral reef area. Where many fish had been swimming about, soon there were few. Nearly all of the client fish had swum away, and the few that remained became sickly. It seems that they could not stay strong and well without their helpful little partners.

3

Well-Paid Protectors

IF YOU EVER get into trouble, it is nice to have someone to protect you. A big brother can keep a bully from hurting you. A policeman protects you and your family from thieves that might try to rob you.

In the animal world too, the weak and the young need protection if they are to survive. A mother lion will fight with fangs and claws to defend her helpless cubs. A mother grouse, a small bird related to the chicken, has no weapons to defend her babies, but she protects them in a different way. If a threatening animal, such as a fox, comes close, she quickly calls to her chicks to be quiet. Then she rushes away from the nest, hopping about and making so much noise that the fox will follow her and not notice her young. In this way the mother grouse risks her own life to protect her chicks.

Sometimes defenseless animals are protected by different kinds of animals, which are not at all related to them. Just as policemen and firemen are paid for protecting citizens, these animal protectors benefit in various ways.

On the warm seas of the world floats the Portuguese man-of-war—one of Nature's most beautiful creatures. Looking like a brilliant blue balloon shimmering in the bright sun, it lazily bobs along in the ocean currents. Sometimes a puff of wind comes along to speed it on its way, much as it does a sailboat with billlowing sails. Many years ago, men of the sea named this lovely creature after the trim Portuguese ships of the day.

This peaceful-looking animal, a relative of the jellyfish, is very well-named, for it is indeed a man-of-war. Trailing in the water beneath its innocent-seeming blue "sail," the Portuguese man-of-war has an arsenal of weapons—dangerous poisoned stingers, studded along slim tentacles that may stretch downward for as much as several yards. A swimmer must beware—if he should touch this deadly beauty, he may be stung again and again.

For a man, a meeting with a Portuguese man-of-war is a very painful experience. But for a fish, such an encounter often ends in death. For that is how the man-of-war catches its dinner. Few fish can survive its poisonous stings.

It seems strange indeed that one kind of small fish, Nomeus, actually makes its home in the tangle of tentacles dangling from the man-of-war. This brightly colored little fish dodges freely in and out among the trailing tentacles. In some mysterious way, which scientists do not yet understand, Nomeus does not seem to be bothered by the deadly stingers of the man-of-war.

Nomeus is a very small, defenseless fish. If it did not have a place to hide, it might be gobbled up by larger fish.

As Nomeus darts about in the sparkling waters, its bright colors attract the attention of many other fish. In a moment one is in pursuit, sure that it will soon be catching a tasty morsel. But then Nomeus darts in among the dangerous tentacles of the man-of-war. If the pursuer follows, it will be lured to its death. For as it brushes against the tentacles, it is stung again and again. Soon the Portuguese man-of-war is eating its prey. Small bits and pieces float away in the water, and Nomeus gobbles them down. In this way the little fish and its protector can both enjoy a meal.

Lured in by Nomeus, a larger fish meets its death in the tentacles of the Portuguese man-of-war.

In the Pacific, we find other strange partnerships. One of them is between the sea anemone, which is a relative of the Portuguese man-of-war, and the damselfish. The tiny damselfish is very pretty, with its bright orange and black body, banded with broad white stripes. But this little fish, like Nomeus, would not long survive if it did not have a place to hide.

Sea anemones look as lovely and innocent as the flower for which they are named. Their barrel-shaped bodies are topped by crowns of waving, petal-like tentacles. These flower-like animals are often beautifully colored— red, orange, green, blue, or various combinations of colors. They live in warm coastal waters, clinging to rocks or half-buried timbers on the ocean bottom.

Within their delicate beauty lurks danger. For the petal-like tentacles carry poisoned stingers, very much like the stingers of the Portuguese man-of-war. And at the center of the "flower" is a gaping mouth. If an unwary fish or other sea creature ventures too close to a sea anemone, it is paralyzed or stung to death. Then the tentacles grip it and haul it in to the sea anemone's open mouth.

Many different sea creatures fall prey to the poisoned stingers of sea anemones. But a damselfish not only can swim about unharmed among their tentacles, but can even dart into the mouth of one and hide in its stomach. The strong juices that can digest much larger fish do not flow when the little damselfish is in the sea anemone's stomach.

This strange partnership works very well. The damselfish comes dashing into its haven whenever a bigger fish threatens it. If the bigger fish follows, it is stung by thousands of poison darts. Then the damselfish and its flower-like partner share in the meal that the little fish has lured "home."

Some damselfish take very good care of their sea anemones. Occasionally skin divers have seen one of these little fish carrying bits of food to its partner and unloading them among the tentacles. Sometimes a sea anemone gets sick, because the water in which it is living has become stale. There is no longer enough oxygen in it. The sea anemone cannot easily move away, for it usually remains firmly anchored to the ocean bottom. But its damselfish companion may fan back and forth with its fins, thus stirring the water and freshening it.

Sea anemones can also form associations with other

Brightly marked damselfish hide among the tentacles of sea anemones.

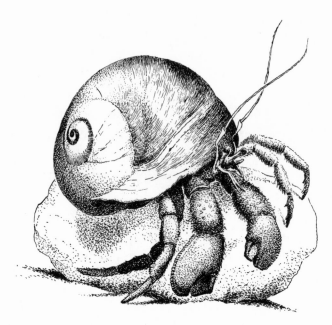

A hermit crab in his borrowed shell

kinds of animals, such as hermit crabs. The hermit crab is a soft-bodied sea creature something like a small lobster. Unlike the lobster, the hermit crab does not have a tough shell of its own. It crawls inside an empty shell, which once belonged to a snail or some other sea animal, and in this way finds protection for its soft body parts. As the hermit crab grows, it cannot make its shell larger, as a living snail can do. Soon the shell is too tight, and the hermit crab must go looking for a new house.

Hermit crabs often decorate their shells with a sort of living camouflage. Sometimes one gently strokes the sides of a sea anemone's barrel-like body until it lets go of the rock to which it is attached. Then the crab carefully lifts the sea anemone onto its shell and holds it there until the tentacled creature has a firm grip. Now the sea anemone can ride about on the crab's back.

There is much to be gained for both partners now. The enemies of the hermit crab find it hard to see it under its flower-like disguise. The sea anemone also protects the crab, stinging any enemies that venture too close. The sea anemone has a much better chance of catching food than its stay-at-home relatives, since the crab carries it about to different parts of the sea. And as the crab tears and eats its own prey, bits of food drift through the water to its anemone companion.

The two partners work so well together that when the hermit crab outgrows its shell, it is careful to move its sea anemone onto the new shell it selects.

Some hermit crabs carry sea anemones on their claws. It is almost like carrying a pair of guns. For if the crab meets an enemy or prey, it can put out one of its tentacle-tipped claws and protect itself or gain a meal.

4

Helpers
Within

THE WORLD about us is swarming with life. The people
walking down the street, the birds flying through the air,
and the animals and plants living in the seas and forests
—these are just the forms of life that we can see. But
there is also a world of life about us that we cannot ordi-
narily see. In the soil that we walk upon, in the water
that we drink, in the air that we breathe, live fantastic
numbers of creatures so tiny that we can see them only
with a microscope. Indeed, until good microscopes
were made, scientists did not know that they existed.
These tiny living things are bacteria, viruses, and other
creatures of many kinds and shapes.

Even inside our bodies, there are swarms of microscopic living creatures. Some of them are dangerous.
Some bacteria and viruses cause diseases such as colds

and measles, as well as the infections that might develop from a cut. Tiny one-celled animals called protozoa occasionally live inside us and make us ill. Malaria, a disease that strikes millions of people each year, is caused by protozoa.

The bacteria that swarm inside us are of many different types. Some are shaped like little rods, others like round balls that float about alone or are joined together in long chains or clumps.

Many of these bacteria do not harm us at all—in fact, some of them help us. Millions and millions of bacteria within our intestines live peacefully on the left-over food that we cannot use. Usually we do not realize that they are there. Yet these intestinal microflora, as they are called, multiply in such enormous numbers that they often make up a large fraction of the contents of our large intestines.

Some of the intestinal flora make chemicals called vitamins—far more than they need for themselves. The extra vitamins, especially the different kinds of B vita-

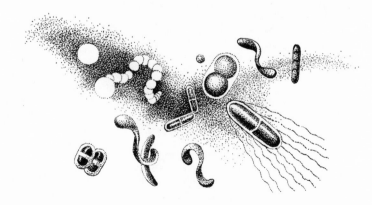

Microscopic organisms that live in the bodies of animals

mins and vitamin K, are used by our bodies to keep us healthy and strong. Doctors have found that after they give a patient a large dose of antibiotics, they often have to prescribe a vitamin supplement. For the antibiotics kill not only the disease bacteria, but also the helpful intestinal flora. Until the patient has a new colony of symbiotic bacteria making vitamins for him, he must take in extra B and K vitamins with his food.

Many other animals—and even plants—have smaller creatures living within their bodies which are helpful to them.

A cow would starve to death in a meadow full of grass if it did not have helpful bacteria living in its stomach. Like the bacteria in our intestines, they make special chemicals. One of these helps to break down grass into simple foods that the cow can digest.

The cow's microflora help her digest grass.

Without these bacteria, the cow could not get much nourishment from the grass that it eats. Grass is made up of cells, which contain many nourishing things, such as fats and proteins, vitamins and minerals, but these food substances are locked inside the cells by a tough wall made of a material called cellulose. The bacteria in the cow's stomach break down cellulose, changing it into simple sugars that the cow can use for energy. When the cell walls are broken down, the cow's own digestive juices go to work on all the other foods that were locked inside.

Cellulose is an important part of wood, too. As you may know, insects called termites eat wood. Termites are pale little creatures. Some people call them "white ants," but actually there is an easy way to tell a termite from an ant. An ant has a very thin waist, while a termite's waist is thick.

Great swarms of termites make nests in or near wood, inside trees or the frames of people's houses. Although people do not like to have them eating away at the frames of houses, termites do an important job in the forest, breaking down old dead logs and branches. But strangely, although much of wood is made up of cellulose, termites cannot digest cellulose all by themselves. Like the cow, these small insects have even smaller creatures living inside them. The smaller creatures are not bacteria. Instead they are microscopic one-celled protozoa—very tiny animals of a type that scientists call flagellates because they swim about with lashing tails called flagella. The flagellates that live inside a termite's intestines, like the bacteria that live in a cow's stomach, break down cellulose into simpler chemicals called sug-

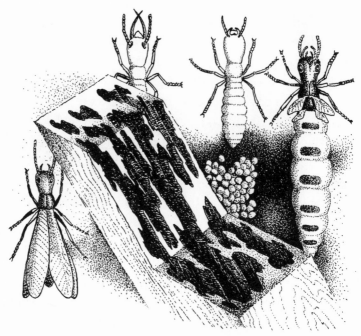

Different types of termites make up a colony.

ars. Then the termite's body can use these sugars for nourishment.

Scientists have found that termites and their flagellates cannot live without each other. Without the shelter and food that they find inside the bodies of their hosts, the little protozoa die. And if the termites are exposed to high temperatures or high pressures of oxygen, treatments that kill the flagellates but do not harm the insects, the termites slowly starve to death. Without their symbiotic partners, they cannot digest the wood they eat.

Termites have a special problem that cows do not have. Once a cow has swallowed a few of the cellulose-digesting bacteria, they begin to grow and multiply in its stomach. Soon it has a thriving colony of bacteria, which it will keep all its life. But termites, like all insects, have to shed their tough skins several times during their lives. Their skins are like armor, and do not give them any room to grow. When a termite sheds its skin, it also loses the whole inside lining of its digestive system, from its mouth down through its intestines. And with its old skin, it loses its whole colony of protozoa. How can it live now? The termite does a very strange—but very fortunate—thing. As soon as it has wriggled out of its outgrown skin, it eats that skin right up, protozoa and all.

We do not have any of the right kind of microscopic creatures to digest cellulose for us. We could eat pounds and pounds of grass and gain almost no nourishment from it at all.

Some animals and plants have small creatures living within them that actually make food for them. The giant bear's-paw clam of the South Pacific lives in sunlit shallow waters. This giant clam may grow to be a yard wide. It spends much of its time with its shells gaping open, and the soft part of its body, called the mantle, facing upward. Sunlight shines into small holes in the clam's mantle, and there, within small pockets in its body, grow microscopic one-celled plants, called green algae.

All green plants make their own food. Algae do this too; they need raw materials, especially water, carbon dioxide, and nitrogen compounds, all of which they can get from the clam's body. They also need energy, which they obtain from the sunlight that streams in through the "skylights" in the clam's mantle. By a process that

In sunlit waters the giant bear's-paw clam raises an algae "garden."

scientists call photosynthesis, the algae capture some of the sunlight energy. They use it to turn the simple chemicals—water, carbon dioxide, and salts—into sugars, starches, and other complicated food chemicals. In their shelter within the clam's body, the algae grow so abundantly that the clam can "harvest" some of them and so satisfy its needs for food, without seriously harming its colony of algae.

Green algae also grow within the bodies of other types of animal partners. In both fresh and salt waters, scientists have found small green flatworms. One type, called Convoluta, is so common off the channel coast of France that the enormous masses of them color the water green. When scientists tried to raise these flatworms in the laboratory, they made some surprising discoveries. These green flatworms do not need to eat anything! And the eggs that they lay, as well as the young that hatch from them, are not green at all—they are almost colorless.

By studying the flatworms in the sea, the scientists discovered that the young eat many microscopic bits of life, including small green algae that are very common in the shallow waters and wet sand in which the flatworms live. Strangely, once the algae get inside the flatworm's body, they are not digested like ordinary food. Instead, these microscopic green plants travel through the animal's body until they settle down, just under its skin. Now the flatworm looks quite green.

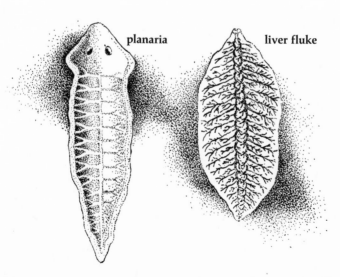

planaria   liver fluke

Unlike its free-living relative the planaria, the parasitic liver fluke has little else but digestive and reproductive organs.

As the sunlight shines upon the worm's thin skin, the algae inside receive energy, which they use to make their own food by photosynthesis. These minute green plants get all the raw materials they need from the flatworm's body. The partnership is also very profitable for the flatworm. Eventually it can stop feeding altogether and live by "harvesting" some of its algae.

But even more important is the exchange of chemicals between the two partners. Flatworms such as one called Convoluta have no special system to get rid of their harmful body wastes, as we do. But the algae that live within them take in these body wastes and turn them into chemicals useful to the flatworm.

In addition, one of the "waste products" of the algae's photosynthesis is oxygen gas. The algae living inside the flatworm's body produce so much oxygen that the worm does not have to depend upon the water in which it lives to get a supply of this important gas to breathe. Scientists have tried experiments in which green flatworms like Convoluta were placed in tightly covered jars

Bean plants: members of the legume family

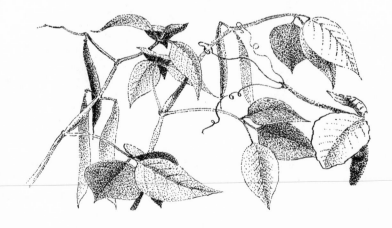

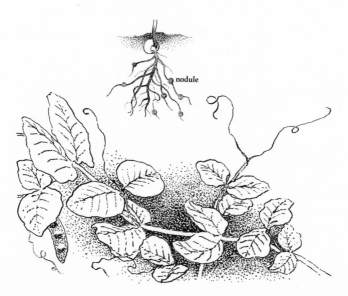

nodule

Peas, like other legumes, get nitrates from bacteria living in nodules on their roots.

CO. SCHOOLS
C719119

of sea water. If the jar was kept in the dark, the worms soon died. But if the jar was placed in sunlight, the worms continued to live for weeks.

Animals are not the only forms of life that can have smaller symbiotic partners living within them. Plants that belong to the legume family, which includes peas and beans, also have small creatures, in this case bacteria, living within them. The bacteria live in special compartments in the roots of the plants. These compartments, called nodules, look like clusters of little balls, clinging to the roots.

Plants usually make their own food. But like algae and all the other green plants, pea and bean plants need certain raw materials. They must have carbon dioxide, a gas they get from the air; they need water and minerals, which their roots take in from the soil. The plants

35

must also take in special salts that contain the element nitrogen. There is nitrogen in the air we breathe, but this is not a form of nitrogen that plants can use. The nitrogen in the air is a gas. The nitrogen that plants can use must be bound up with other elements in special ways, in salts called nitrates. There are some bacteria in the soil that turn nitrogen gas from the air into salts such as nitrates. But sometimes there are not enough of these bacteria. If there is not enough nitrate in the soil, farmers must add nitrate fertilizers, so that their crops will grow healthy and strong.

But pea and bean plants that have symbiotic bacteria living in their nodules do not need to get their nitrates from the soil. The nodule bacteria take nitrogen gas from air pockets in the soil and bind it with other elements to form salts that the plants can use. These bacteria are called nitrogen-fixing bacteria. In their partnership with pea and bean plants, these bacteria gain shelter; they also get sugars and oxygen, which they need for their activities.

The nodule bacteria bind so much nitrogen that they enrich the soil. Farmers often take advantage of this effect by a practice called crop rotation. After harvesting corn or some other crop that takes nitrates out of the soil without putting any back, the farmer may plant a crop of peas, beans, or some other plant with nodules. They leave the soil rich in nitrates, which can be used by later crops such as corn.

5

Farmers
and
Herders

AMONG THE STRANGEST symbiotic relationships that naturalists have discovered in fields and forests are those of the insect farmers. Some beetles, termites, and ants grow gardens and gather harvests to feed themselves and their families. Just like human farmers, these insect farmers tirelessly care for their crops, and without them the plants might not survive. But unlike human farmers, these insects have their farms underground. And their crops are not green at all—they are pale, whitish plants called fungi. A mushroom is a kind of fungus, and so is the mold that grows on a stale piece of bread.

In the tropical forests of the Americas, one often finds a parade of ants, crawling up and down a tree. Each ant coming down holds over its head, like a little parasol, a bit of green leaf that it has cut from the tree.

These are leafcutter ants. Each has a large pair of sharp jaws, which it uses like a pair of shears to snip off pieces of leaves. Up and down the tree trunk they go, in an endless procession. As some ants carry their leaf burdens down to the ground, others climb up to gather more. Soon the whole tree may be stripped bare of its leaves.

What do the ants want with all these leaves? Naturalists thought at first that they gather the leaves for food. But this is not the case at all. Careful observation revealed that each ant carries its bit of leaf down deep into the ground. There thousands of worker ants of the leafcutter colony, each carrying a grain of earth at a time, have dug out caverns that extend down to fifteen feet below the surface and stretch out several yards wide. In such a cavern, vast indeed in comparison with the tiny insects, other members of the ant colony now chew the leaves into a spongy mash. This they lay down on the floor of the cavern to form a bed on which they grow their fungus garden.

Leafcutter ants gather leaves for their underground fungus farms.

The little ant farmers spread their plants on top of the spongy leaf bed. The leafcutter ants work as hard as any human farmer to keep their fungus plants growing healthy and strong. They dig and chew the spongy leaf mash and keep weed fungi from choking out their crop. As the fungi grow, they form round balls, like miniature heads of cauliflower. The ants harvest these fungus balls to feed themselves and their young.

When a queen ant leaves the nest to start a new colony somewhere else, she takes bits of the fungus along with her, neatly packed away in a special pouch in her mouth. These will be the "seeds" for the new crop. And in this way, both the ants and their fungi can spread to new territories.

The leafcutter ants are not the only ant farmers. Other kinds of ants raise animals, very much as human farmers raise livestock. They keep little "ant cows," which are really insects called aphids. Aphids feed on plants, sucking juices from stems or leaves or roots. And the aphids make a sweet juice of their own, called honey-dew.

The ants love honeydew, and they take tender care of their aphid "cows" so that they will have a ready supply. Some ants carry their aphids through long underground tunnels to place them on the roots of corn or grasses. Other ants bring their aphids outdoors to "pasture" each day on leaves or stems. Somehow the ants seem to know exactly which part of which kind of plant will be just right for the particular kind of aphid they are raising.

Human farmers have a very good reason for wanting to know more about the ant "cow raisers." Aphids do a great deal of damage to corn and other crops. Researchers from agricultural colleges and government agencies are studying how ants and aphids live in the fields. They also raise ants and aphids in their laboratories. In this way scientists are discovering some amazing things about these strange insect partnerships.

The ant "dairy farmers" milk their aphid "cows" in a way that is surprisingly similar to the way human farmers milk their cows. The ant farmer goes up to each aphid in turn and strokes it gently. Out squirts a drop of the sugary honeydew. Quickly the ant catches the drop in its mouth and swallows it into a special storage compartment in the front of its stomach. When it has enough, it carries the sweet juice back to the nest.

Some ant herders build shelters for their aphid "cows"

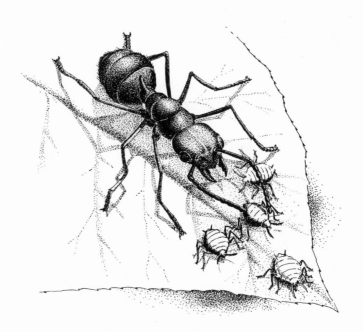

An ant "dairy farmer" milks his aphid "cow."

to shield them from the rain. Ants will also fight to protect their herds from enemies. (There are even some "cattle rustlers" in the ant world.)

When the days grow colder, the aphids lay tough-walled eggs to last over the winter. Their ant herders carefully gather these eggs and store them away in the ant-nests until spring.

The partnership between the ant farmers and their aphid "cows" is a happy affair for both. The aphid is fed and cared for and protected; the ant receives sweet, nourishing food in return.

6

Teamwork
in Fields
and Gardens

IF YOU WALK through a park or field on a warm summer day, or even pass by a weed-covered vacant lot, you will see swarms of insects buzzing and fluttering about. Black-and-gold bees and bright-winged butterflies flit from flower to flower. They stop at each flower for a moment, and then fly on.

Naturalists have discovered that these insects, gathering food, are actually aiding the plants, too, by helping to spread their pollen to other plants of the same kind. Through long hours of watching and observing, in the fields and in the laboratories, these scientists have learned many fascinating details about pollination. The research is still going on, and each year new facts are learned.

It has been found that to make seeds, which will grow

into new plants, most flowers need some help. Before a seed can be formed, a tiny male germ cell called a sperm must join with a small female cell called an egg. The sperm cells are found inside grains of pollen, which are formed in flower parts called stamens. These are long, thread-like structures capped by a cluster of pollen sacs, called the anther. In each pollen sac there are many pollen grains. And inside each pollen grain there are cells that develop into sperm cells. The eggs of the flower are formed in a different part of the flower, called the pistil. The pistil grows right in the middle of the flower, surrounded by a number of stamens, and it usually has the shape of a vase. The eggs are formed near the bottom of the pistil, in the rounded part called the ovary.

Bees gathering food help to pollinate flowers.

When pollen grains land on the sticky top of the pistil, called the stigma, each grain begins to grow a thin tube, which pushes downward, toward the eggs below. As the tube grows longer, a minute sperm cell from within the pollen grain travels down inside it. When the tip of the tube reaches the eggs inside the ovary, the sperm joins with an egg, and the life of a new plant is begun.

The transfer of the pollen from anther to stigma is called pollination. And the joining of sperm and egg is known as fertilization.

A few kinds of flowers are able to bring their sperms and eggs together without any help. But most kinds need some aid in pollination.

Some flowers depend on the wind to carry their pollen through the air, sometimes for miles, to another flower of the same type. Plants that depend upon the wind for pollination make amazingly large amounts of light, fluffy pollen. If you suffer from hay fever, you probably know that the air is filled with billions and billions of grains of ragweed pollen at certain times of the year. The wind carries pollen in all directions—over fields and rivers, over rooftops, through open windows, and even into people's noses. Only a very few of the pollen grains actually reach another flower of the same kind.

For many plants there are surer ways of carrying the pollen to the stigma. Insects such as bees, beetles, butterflies, moths, and ants help some plants to reproduce themselves by carrying pollen from one flower to another. Flowers of other plants may be pollinated by birds or even bats.

Of course, animal pollinators do not really plan to take the pollen from one flower along to another. They are gathering food for themselves, and they carry pollen on their bodies without meaning to at all. For instance, the busy honeybee flits from flower to flower, always stopping at flowers of the same kind, on her journey from the hive. As she stops to sip some nectar, pollen from the anthers of the flowers brushes off onto tiny hairs on her body. Or she may be filling the special pollen bags on her legs with pollen to be made into beebread, and soon she is covered with the dusty pollen from head to foot. Then when she lands on another flower, some of the pollen that she has picked up falls off onto its stigma.

Flowers are wonderfully suited to the animals that pollinate them. Bats fly at night, and the flowers that bats visit often stay tightly shut during the day, opening only in the evening. Flowers that moths pollinate also usually open in the late afternoon or twilight, when the moths are beginning to be about.

Scientists have found that bees can see many colors very well, but have trouble telling red from green. And, as you might expect, flowers visited by bees are usually yellow or blue, but hardly ever red. (The few red flowers that do attract bees usually reflect ultraviolet light, too, which we cannot see but bees can.) These flowers also have a sweet odor that the bees can smell as they fly by, and sugary nectar for them to sip.

Flowers that appeal to butterflies also smell sweet, but they have colors that butterflies see very well, mostly red and orange. Birds have wonderfully keen eyesight, but do not smell very well. The flowers that they visit are usually large and bright, but have little odor.

Even the shape of the flowers is amazingly suited to

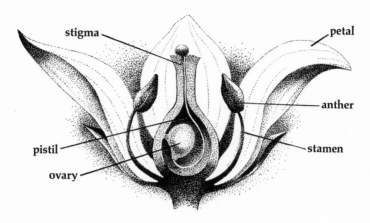

Flower parts

just the kind of animals that pollinate them. Only the long, slim bill of the hummingbird can reach the sweet nectar at the bottom of the tube-shaped flowers that it visits. The petals of flowers to which bees are attracted usually are shaped like a sort of landing platform, which makes it easy for the bee to land.

Flowers that beetles visit often have petals that form a wide, shallow cup. The beetle may crawl up and eat parts of the flower—not only nectar and pollen, but the petals too! But as it rests there, munching away, pollen it has carried along from other flowers falls onto the pistil, and the stamens dust down a new supply onto the beetle's back. In fact, some flowers act like spring traps, with stamens that snap over and dust a load of pollen down onto any insect that brushes against the flower.

Most flowers could never make seeds without their animal pollinators. These animals, in turn, might starve to death without the sweet and nourishing food provided by the flowers.

46

7

One-Sided
Relationships

WE HAVE SEEN that the world is full of creatures that
live and work together, for the benefit of both. But
there are many cases of associations in the living world
where one member seems to receive all the gain, while
the other does not seem to be helped. These are cases
of commensalism. In other cases one member may
even be harmed. These are cases of parasitism.

All the diseases caused by bacteria, viruses, and microscopic protozoa are examples of parasitism. The
minute parasite lives within the body of its host and
draws nourishment from it, without giving anything in
return. The parasite grows and multiplies, and eventually the strain on the host may become so great that it
becomes ill or even dies. Microscopic parasites afflict
man and very likely all other animals as well. Even

47

plants can develop diseases caused by germs and other parasites.

Not all disease-causing parasites are microscopic. Both animals and plants may be bothered by fungus growths. Worms such as hookworms, pinworms, and tapeworms live inside the bodies of people and animals. These parasites are not microscopic at all—a tapeworm may grow to as much as 60 feet long! It could hardly fit inside the body of its host if it were not so thin and flat. The tapeworm looks something like a long tape measure—it has a small head and a body made up of almost a thousand segments. Each segment can give rise to new tapeworms. For like many parasites, the tapeworm is so well adapted to its way of life that it has lost all the body parts it does not need. All it can do is feed and reproduce. But it does this so well that a single adult tapeworm can produce more than a million eggs a day.

Animals such as cows and pigs often take in tapeworm eggs with unclean food. The eggs hatch inside their intestines, and the young tapeworms make their way through the bloodstream of the animal to its muscles. There they settle down and may be transferred to humans who kill the animal and eat its meat. In the intestines of their new hosts, the tapeworms grow into adults. They eat so much food that their human host

Coiled inside a man's body, a tapeworm can grow as long as 60 feet.

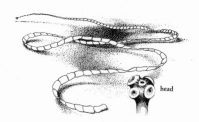

head

often becomes thin and ill. These worms also make harmful chemicals, which poison their host. There are medicines that can be taken to kill tapeworm parasites, but it is best to avoid getting them at all by not eating meat that has not been thoroughly cooked.

Some parasites live on the outside of the bodies of their hosts. Fleas and ticks cling to animals' skin and suck their blood. Fish parasites called lampreys have

Life cycle of the malaria organism

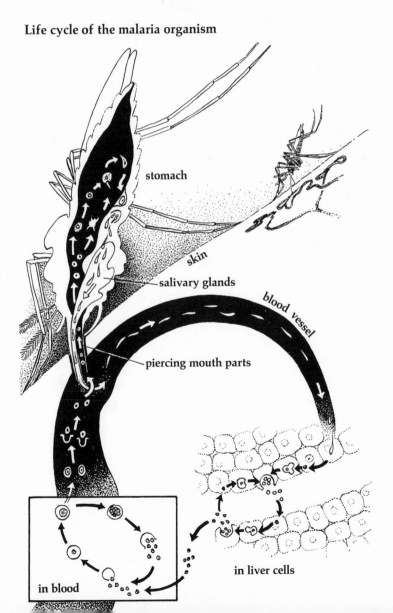

stomach

skin

salivary glands

blood vessel

piercing mouth parts

in liver cells

in blood

A parasitic lamprey sucks the blood of a lake trout.

mouths specially adapted to act as suction cups, with which they cling to other fish and suck blood from them. After lampreys found their way into the Great Lakes, these parasites killed off many valuable food fish, such as lake trout. The fishing industry is studying the habits of the lamprey very closely, trying to find ways to get rid of this harmful pest.

Some parasites have quite different hosts at different times of their lives. The protozoan that causes malaria, for example, spends part of its life in the body of a mosquito. It is transferred to man or some other animal through a mosquito bite.

Malaria is a serious worldwide problem. It afflicts hundreds of millions of humans and causes millions of deaths each year. Since the discovery of DDT and other insecticides, man has succeeded in reducing the mosquito problem and as a result has sharply reduced the number of cases of malaria. But this disease still remains one of the major causes of sickness and death in the world.

Small parasitic worms called Chinese liver flukes have an even more complicated life than the malaria protozoan. Eggs from these worms pass into the intestines of their human host, and then out of the body. But in Japan and China, where the liver fluke is common, human wastes are used for fertilizer. From fields and rice paddies, the eggs of the flukes are washed into rivers and streams, where they are eaten by snails. The eggs hatch and grow inside the bodies of the snails until they are released as small swimming forms. If one of these forms meets a fish, it burrows under the fish's scales and curls up in a tough, protective coat called a cyst. In the Orient, it is very common for people to eat raw fish. If the raw fish contains liver fluke cysts, the worms grow in the person's body, eventually producing eggs of their own to start the cycle over again.

Liver flukes are an important problem in the Far East. They live in the livers of their human hosts and feed on their blood. And so, these parasites weaken their hosts, who are then much more likely to catch other diseases as well.

All through the kingdoms of life there are one-sided relationships—far more than the cases of symbiosis in which both partners benefit. But fortunately, even in one-sided relationships, there are numerous cases when the member that does not gain is not really harmed either—the association does not seem to make much difference to him. These are cases of commensalism. Often they are casual associations, easily broken, and not really vital even to the organism that benefits from them. But in some cases where scientists now believe that only one partner is helped, the other may actually benefit too, in some way we do not yet understand.

For example, green algae grow on the thick fur of some land-dwelling sloths. The algae gain a place in the sun. But what does the sloth gain? Scientists are not sure. Many of them say that the sloth does not really gain anything. Some scientists, however, believe that the green algae, which grow so thickly that the sloth seems to have green fur, help to hide it from its enemies. For its green coat blends with the leaves in the forest.

Some animals seek a free ride in life, like hitchhikers that try to get from place to place without paying for their transportation. Others may find a free home, which they neither build nor help to keep up. Let us find out more about the creatures that gain benefits from others without paying for them with some service.

Sharks are among the fiercest of the fish in the sea. With their slashing teeth, they can kill almost any other fish, and some sharks even attack giant whales. It appears, though, that these ferocious creatures do not mind carrying certain other fish around with them as passengers. These are the remoras, or sucker fish.

Algae may grow in the thick fur of the sloth.

Remoras use their suckers to get a free ride from a shark.

Remoras are long, eel-like fish, each with a powerful sucker on top of its head. With this sucker it can attach itself so firmly to a fish that it cannot be pulled off. The sucker fish does not suck the shark's blood as a lamprey would, or hurt it in any way. It simply uses its sucker to get a free ride. If the remora sees a tasty-looking small fish swimming nearby as it is being whisked along by the shark, the sucker fish lets go to swim over and catch its meal. Sometimes the remora gets a free meal along with its free ride. For when the shark catches a fish and greedily devours it, the remora can feast on the scraps that drift about in the water.

Remoras sometimes attach themselves not only to sharks of many kinds, but also to turtles, dolphins, whales, or even to ships passing by. Strangely, though the remora will hitch a ride whenever it can, it swims swiftly and gracefully on its own.

But there are other hitchhikers of the sea who cannot swim at all. If you go down to the seashore and look at the pilings of an old pier near the low tide line, you

53

may find barnacles growing on the wood. These are small cup-shaped shells, with feathery legs that poke out from the tops of the cups and swish in tiny sea creatures from the water. When barnacles are young, they swim about freely, and look something like small lobsters. In fact, they belong to the same family as the lobsters. But once they grow up, they settle down on a rock or piling, and never move again.

Some barnacles settle down on moving objects, such as the hulls of swiftly moving ships. There they become a great problem to shippers, for tons and tons of barnacles may build up on a single large ship. The growths of barnacles are so bulky and uneven that they prevent the water from slipping smoothly along the sides of the ship. They act as a drag on it and slow it down. Enormous amounts of money must be spent by shippers each year to burn and scrape barnacles off their ships.

Some barnacles even attach themselves to other living creatures of the sea. Barnacles may settle down on the backs of turtles, on the shells of snails or clams, or on the bodies of fish and whales, and grow there, never to move on their own again. There are even barnacles that live on the barnacles that live on the bodies of whales.

The life of a barnacle on a swimmer has many benefits for the barnacle. Its cousins who stay on rocks or pilings can get only the food that drifts to them through the sea. But the barnacles that travel on a swiftly moving whale or fish or ship have miles and miles of ocean to feed from. And, like the remora, they do not seem to hurt their chauffeur.

In addition to the creatures that gain a free ride from other creatures, there are animals which settle down in a shelter built and maintained by a different kind of animal. They contribute nothing, and they may even share some of their host's food. But they do not do any real harm.

Ants are tireless workers, who build large nests and keep them neat and tidy. They work together to gather food and care for their young. Many creatures take advantage of the hard-working ants. Some crickets, as well as roaches, beetles, and spiders, move right into the ants' homes and live there. The ants do not seem to mind them. The animals that share the ants' nests certainly benefit—they have shelter and sometimes make off with a meal or two when the ants are not looking.

There are many other cases in nature where animals share a home built by the labor of another. Some beetles live in the burrows of meadow mice. The mice do not seem to pay any attention to the beetles, and the beetles probably do help somewhat to keep the burrows clean by eating bits and scraps that the mice leave lying about.

A large hawk called the osprey builds an enormous nest by piling up branches and stones. This giant nest often becomes a bird "apartment house." On the top floor lives the osprey. In various nooks and crannies lower in the pile, smaller birds such as grackles, wrens, and sparrows build their nests. They do not bother the osprey, and it does not bother them, for this fierce hawk eats mainly fish, which it catches in the water nearby. The smaller birds get a double benefit—they gain not only shelter, but also protection from their enemies, who are afraid to come too near the hawk.

In the sea many creatures share the homes of others.

One fat worm that lives off the California coast builds a large, U-shaped tunnel in the mud at the sea bottom. So many other creatures share this burrow that the worm is called the "innkeeper." Crabs and clams live there, and so do other kinds of worms, which steal a bit of food whenever they can. Small fish take shelter just inside the entrance of the tunnel. They take no food from their "innkeeper," but do find a safe place to hide from their enemies.

One of the strangest homes shared by many sea creatures is the body of a large sponge. Probably most of the sponges you use for washing dishes or in the bathtub are made of plastic. But perhaps you have also seen a real sponge. It is the dried skeleton of an animal that grows in the sea.

The sponge has many little pores and passageways throughout its body, through which water flows. These passageways are lined with cells equipped with tiny whip-like structures called flagella, which beat back and forth and set up currents in the water. The sponge strains out tiny bits of food from the currents of water flowing through the passages in its body. But these passageways also make a fine home for many other sea creatures. Frequently shrimps and worms, and even small fish, find shelter there.

8

Symbiosis
All About

WE HAVE LEARNED that many different creatures in our world help each other to find food and shelter and protection from their enemies.

But there is one animal that has far more relationships with different kinds of creatures, both animals and plants, than any other. This is man himself.

When a farmer plants a crop in the fields, he is helping the plants to survive. He enriches the soil with fertilizer. As the seedlings grow, he waters them, sometimes with special irrigation ditches. He removes the weeds so that the growing plants will not be choked. Without the constant care of the farmer these plants would not grow as well. In fact, there are some plants that cannot grow at all without a farmer's care. Seedless oranges and grapes, for instance, cannot reproduce by themselves. The farmer cuts off a small branch from a seedless orange tree and grafts it to a young orange tree of a different kind. He places the cut end of the branch in a cut in the tree and binds the two together until they actually grow together. The small branch now becomes part of the young tree. When the tree is ready to bear fruit, it will bear seedless oranges.

The farmer, of course, benefits enormously when he grows crops. He has food for his family to eat and goods to sell at the market. Farmers also gain from partnerships with animals, such as cattle and sheep, chickens and pigs. The farmer feeds and shelters and protects his livestock, and from them he obtains food and other goods to sell at the market.

Farmers are not the only humans who have partnerships with animals and plants. Everyone who has a pet dog or cat is living symbiotically with that animal. The human provides food, shelter, care, and love. The animal returns this affection. In addition, it may also work by catching mice or protecting the house from thieves and prowlers.

Not all the creatures that live with man are welcome. Mice, rats, and cockroaches find food and shelter in houses, barns, and even ships built by man. The relationship is quite one-sided. These pests do no good, and in fact cause a great deal of damage by eating and spoiling food and goods; they also spread diseases.

Certain kinds of plants, too, cause harm to man and his possessions. Molds and mildews ruin his food, clothes, and books, and some forms may even rot away the timbers of his house. Tree roots crack his pave-

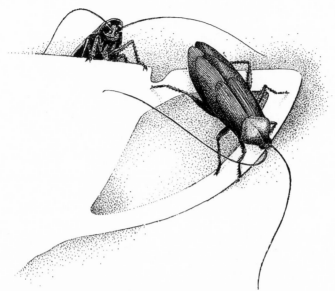

Roaches and other insects are uninvited guests in man's homes.

ments, and weeds constantly threaten to overrun his gardens.

In your own home and in the neighborhood about, you can find many examples of symbiosis. If you look closely at your pet cat or dog you may discover fleas in its fur. These fleas are parasites. They gain shelter and food, but they hurt their furry hosts by sucking blood and spreading disease.

If there is a vacant lot or field nearby, you can see how bees, butterflies, and other insects visit flowers and help to pollinate them. If you look closely at the leaves and stems of plants, you may find aphids sucking away at the plant juices. These insects may be found on almost any kind of plant. For there are nearly two thousand different kinds of aphids, and each has its own favorite plants. If you are lucky, you may find some aphids that are being cared for by ants. You might even see an ant milking its aphid "cow." Such aphids are actually a part of two different kinds of symbiotic relationships. They are parasites on the plants on which they live, for they harm them by sucking the plant juices. But their relationship with ants is one of mutualism, providing benefits for both.

When you are looking for symbiosis in the natural world around you, you must be very careful. If you rush into a field, or walk noisily through the woods, or splash about in the water, the many living creatures there will scatter before you in every direction. Some will leap away, others will disappear into the grasses or holes in tree trunks, and some will keep so still that you do not even notice them. The wild creatures that you do see may not be acting the way they normally do.

Scientists who study nature have a similar problem. These scientists, who are called naturalists, have worked out special techniques so that they can find out how animals really live. A naturalist going out into a field or forest may lie still for many hours, quietly watching. He may build a blind of branches or grasses in which to hide, as duck hunters do, so that the wild creatures about will not notice him. He may watch through field glasses so that he need not get too close. He may take with him many modern tools, from high-speed cameras to tape recorders.

Naturalists also go into the sea, to watch animals in their watery home, for in an aquarium sea animals might not act as they normally do. Naturalists glide through

shallow waters in glass-bottomed boats, looking down at the busy life below. In deeper waters, skin divers go down to explore the bottom. And scientists are even exploring the ocean depths in bathyscaphes—diving bells with thick walls and windows to look through.

Professional naturalists also learn much about how animals and plants live from observations made by amateur naturalists—people young and old who have made the study of nature a hobby. These amateurs have learned how to watch wild things without frightening them, and how to write or draw exactly what they see.

As an amateur naturalist in your own neighborhood, or in a nearby park or field or forest, you can use many of the same techniques that professional naturalists use. If you want to watch animals, you must learn how to behave so that they do not realize that you are there. Animals have several ways of detecting the presence of a stranger—by sight, sound, or smell. Animals will quickly sense almost any movement. But if you do not move, they can often look right at you and not be disturbed by your presence. If you should suddenly cough, rustle the grasses, or snap a twig, all the animals about may scurry for cover. Some of them have ears so keen that they pick up sounds that we would not even notice. In fact, animals such as field mice communicate with each other with squeaks so high-pitched that our ears cannot hear them at all. In the animal world, the sense of smell is often one of the most important of the senses. Even if you are careful to make no noise and do not move at all, many animals may be able to detect your presence by the odors of your body. Winds and even gentle breezes can carry these odors over great distances.

And so, before you pick a spot to settle down, you must test the wind, and always choose a place where the breezes will carry your odors away from the animals you want to watch.

To be a good amateur naturalist, you must make careful records of what you see. Try to make sketches or take pictures with a camera. Make notes of just how the animal moves or what it eats and how it behaves toward other animals.

Using these techniques, you may discover many fascinating examples of how plants and animals live and grow and work together. You may even make some new discoveries that you can share with other naturalists all around the world.

Index